The Judicial Branch:

Keeping Things Fair

By
Dr. Latina Campbell

Print ISBN: 978-1-966491-10-1

eBook ISBN: 978-1-966491-11-8

Printed in the United States of America

Story Corner Publishing & Consulting, Inc.

Chesapeake, VA 23321

Storycornerpublishing@yahoo.com

www.StoryCornerPublishing.com

Dedication

I dedicate this book to all the children who dream of becoming the future president, members of Congress, judges, lawyers, politicians, law enforcement, or even military.
Be fair and just with everyone and do everything in love and kindness.
Put God first and allow Him to lead you through every decision.

In the meantime, remember no matter who holds office or what laws are passed, God has the final say and remains in control. There's no need to worry about things you see happen in the world, just pray to God. Prayer changes everything.

P.S.

I'm proud of you because you are brave!

Do you know what's fair and what's not so right?

Who makes sure our laws are clear and bright?

There's a branch of government with this special job—

The Judicial Branch, it's really top-notch!

The Judicial Branch is like a referee,

It listens and decides what the law should be.

It checks if rules are fair and just,

So people know what they can trust.

At the very top, where the big decisions go,

There's a special court we all should know.

It's called the Supreme Court, wise and grand,

Nine judges, or justices, take the stand.

These justices wear robes of black,

And hear cases where facts may lack.

They read the law, they ask what's true,

Then decide what's fair for me and you.

LEGISLATION

9

But the Judicial Branch isn't just the top,

There are many more courts where cases stop.

Local courts help in towns and cities,

And state courts listen to big committees.

LAW & JUSTICE

What kinds of questions do judges decide?

Things like, "Did someone break the law?" they'll provide.

Or, "Does this new rule follow the Constitution?"

They solve tough problems with a fair solution.

The Judicial Branch also protects our rights,

Like freedom of speech and peaceful fights.

It checks the laws from Congress, too,

To make sure they're fair for me and you.

Judges don't make laws—that's not their game,

But they explain them so we know the name.

They help us understand what's right and true,

And how the rules apply to you.

17

When people disagree, they turn to the court,

Where judges will listen, debate, and report.

They hear both sides and take their time,

To make decisions that are fair and fine.

The Judicial Branch has one big goal,

To make fairness the heart and soul.

It balances power in our great land,

Working with Congress and the President's hand.

Without the Judicial Branch, what would we do?

Who'd make sure our laws are true?

This branch is here to keep things fair,

Protecting justice everywhere!

So now you know this branch so wise,

It keeps the law under watchful eyes.

The Judicial Branch helps us all get along,

With fairness, justice, and a heart so strong!

The End